WILL SOMEONE LEAD
ME TO A PUB?

I0674409

Copyright © 2017 Read Books Ltd.
This book is copyright and may not be
reproduced or copied in any way without
the express permission of the publisher in writing

British Library Cataloguing-in-Publication Data
A catalogue record for this book is available from the
British Library

. . . I rose politely in the club,
I said : " I feel a little bored ;
Will someone lead me to a Pub ? "

G. K. CHESTERTON.

WILL SOMEONE LEAD ME TO A PUB? Being a Note upon certain of the Taverns, old and new, of London ; Presenting something of their Story, their Company, and their Quiddity. Which may entertain Those at Home, and may cause a Spasm of Nostalgia in the Breasts of Englishmen in the Dominions, the Dependencies, and the lonely Out-posts of our Far-Flung etc., where To-day, as in Kipling's Day, Men sit Swapping Lies about the Purple East, and when they tire of that, talk in the sour-sweet Accents of the Exile, of their Favourite London Bars ; by THOMAS BURKE

WILL SOMEONE LEAD ME TO A PUB?

FROM the days of its foundation the London tavern has suffered many and frequent changes. But it is one of those features of our life, like the Government and the circus, which, the more they change, the more constant they are. Despite the efforts made to abolish it, and, failing that, to harass its functions with a multitude of small laws, it goes on. It adapts itself to the needs of each generation, and is pliant to every new law forced upon it, while remaining in spirit what it was when it first appeared upon the social scene. If the company that made the Tabard, the Boar's Head, the Three Cranes, the Devil or the Mitre; or, later, Ned Ward's King's Head, or Tom Belcher's Daffy Club at the Castle, or Mother Butler's Queen of Bohemia; or, later still, Washington Irving's Half-Moon in Little Britain, or Lamb's Cat and Salutation—if these men could enter a London bar of to-day, they would notice a number of differences in the form of the building and its appointments. They would find some new drinks, and the company would be wearing different dress and using new idioms. But they would find still an atmosphere that they would recognize, and a company that would be in tune with them. They would feel, I think, that the evening which broke off for them a century, or centuries, ago was only just beginning.

For there has been no time in London's story when the tavern wasn't there. It has grown with us from our beginnings, and from Saxon ale-house to modern fake-Tudor saloon, it has been as constant in the London scene as the Lord Mayor or the street-market. It persists, not because the English are a drunken race, but because it serves an occasion served by nothing else. It is not merely an interesting survival, like the curfew of Ely Place, or the Queen Anne costume of our lawyers. It has the same place and meaning in our lives which it had in the lives of our ancestors. It fits the national temper as completely as our unwritten Constitution fits it, and it has survived under criticism as nonchalantly as the English Manner survives.

It almost escapes definition. It is not a

shop for the sale of strong drink. It is not a club. It is a *public*-house, providing drink of various kind, with the atmosphere and some of the amenities of a private house. It is not a necessity, like the Town Hall or the restaurant or the school ; yet London, or any other English town, without it would be as unfinished as if it lacked these other things. Nobody passionately wants it. It is one of those pleasant things—like letters and autumn and bread-and-butter—which we take for granted and would miss if they did not arrive.

It is the one place where a man may meet and talk with strangers on level terms. It is the common and open club, with no rules or formalities of entry save those of. decent behaviour and mutual respect. On the floor of the bar your clothes, your position, your income, go for nothing. Only in the bar can you see, in one easy gathering, rich man, poor man, poet, merchant, soldier, sailor, squire, scholar, tailor, and—perhaps—thief. These types you may also see in trains and tea-shops and hotels. But in these places they are separate; not one gathering of casual affability and chit-chat. Under the roof of the bar are revealed many little aspects and angles of English life and character which

remain wholly unperceived by those whose
principles or tastes forbid them to enter a
bar. Comedy, unsuspected outside, finds here
a sympathetic air in which to breathe. The
flesh-and-soil humour of Chaucer and Shakespeare and Fielding has mostly vanished from
English life and speech. Within the doors of
the tavern it survives, and it has more to
do with English attitude and opinion than
detached students imagine.

One might almost say that nobody can
fully read the English until he has sat with
them in the Blue Goat or Spotted Unicorn.
Many politicians miss their aim at the Englishman because they do not fully know him;
they have never seen him on the ground where
he flowers. To some of them, any man in a
tavern is a low fellow with the drink habit.
Which is as sensible as to conclude that any
man at a dinner-table is a glutton. You do,
of course, find the drunkard in the bar; you
can also find him in famous clubs, in hotels,
and in the rooms of private mansions. Just
as, for sensible people, the purpose of the
dining-room is not over-eating, so the purpose of the bar is not to provide means of
intoxication but to provide a rendezvous, an
atmosphere, in which men may take either

COMEDY FINDS HERE A SYMPATHETIC AIR

fermented drink or an innocent ginger-ale, openly and in surroundings which catch something of the club spirit with less formality than the club proper, and something more in stir and variety of scene and character than any club can give.

Nothing survives without a reason. Abolish the bar and make the chemist's shop the only place where a "drink" can be got—to be consumed at a draught, and exit. The result would be that scarcely one in a thousand of the present customers of the bar would patronize the chemist. Because few of those customers are addicted to drink; at least, no more than women are "addicted" to morning coffee and afternoon tea. Men visit the bar from any one of half a dozen motives. They may have, in their own homes, or in their clubs, better and cheaper drink than they can find in the bar. Still they will prefer, on occasion, to visit a bar, often to take merely a schoolboy lime-juice or barley-water, and to look at a new flash of life, or catch the spirit of a district. They like the atmosphere; the feeling of friendly, common life—using common in its dignified, not its County, sense. There is no other place in which one can fill the odd ten minutes, or take a casual chat

with a chance-encountered friend. To take
him to a tea-shop, or hotel-lounge, and sit
down at a table and wait for service, makes
the thing foolishly formal, and extends the
meeting longer, perhaps, than either desires.

Only in the bar can the poor man living
in London lodgings make a casual escape from
his loneliness. He may join little clubs or
lecture-societies, but they are set affairs with
set meeting-times. He cannot drop in and
find talk. And if you tell me that he might
find casual talk in a tea-shop, I shall retort
that you have clearly never been poor and
lonely, and never have tried to start a conversation at a tea-shop table. The atmosphere
is as congenial to impromptu talk as that of
a Free Library Reading Room or the vault
of a movie-palace. But in the bar he may
almost always find somebody with whom to
exchange a few words. Even if he does not
make conversation he finds a sense of being
part of the affair. Talk and jokes are not
muttered. They are offered at large, and the
unintroduced are free to share the rather
laboured but warm facetiæ which are the
average man's nearest cousinship with wit.
In the bar the Englishman eases his usual
reserve, and the newcomer can be as unbut-

toned as the rest, because he is anonymous. Often two men may meet occasionally in a given bar over the course of a year, and exchange talk, and at the end of the year not know each other's name. It is the one spot in social life where a man may be part of a group, and yet preserve his privacy to the point of being only "the little fat chap", or "the tall fellow", or "the walrus moustache". It is the one social feature which remains with us as Tried and True. We abolish this, and introduce that, and desert the other, but through all destruction and innovation, the tavern stands.

Firmly set as it has been in the masculine social landscape through many centuries, it came, in the nineteenth century, to the horizon of all London men, women, and children. Coaches and short-stages had used the central inns as their starting-places, but the arrival of the omnibus implied many stopping-places, and these were always fixed at taverns. Indeed, the first London omnibus made its first London journey from a tavern (in 1829), and the tavern is still with us—the Yorkshire Stingo, in Marylebone Road. By the diverse ranging of the omnibus, many taverns, formerly known only to the people of their district, became a part of the mental geography of all Londoners. They were landmarks of London travel. Until the coming of the wider-ranging motor-bus, which had no need of troughs and feed-bags, all Londoners, and all who had spent a month in London, had heard of the Elephant and Castle, the Bricklayer's Arms, the Angel (Islington), the Plough (Clapham), the Swiss Cottage, the Adelaide (Chalk Farm), the Crown (Cricklewood), the Nag's Head (Holloway), and the Monster (Pimlico). To-day, though no longer marking the end of a journey, they are still active in their business.

London has no taverns of the structural age and grace of some of our country inns. We have nothing to match the George, at Glastonbury; the Angel, at Grantham; the George, at Norton St. Philip; the Ostrich, at Colnbrook; or the King's Head, at Aylesbury. Of the London houses mentioned by that incredible pub-crawler, Drunken Barnaby, whose journeys are set forth in Braithwaite's queer verses, one only survives. The Mother Red Cap, of Camden Town, is still there, though in late-nineteenth-century shape. In the City, some long-dated places have held their ground, but only by frequent structural changes, or complete rebuilding. The Raglan Arms, near the G.P.O., is said to hold one of the oldest London licences; other long-established houses in later dress are the London Tavern, Fenchurch Street; the Tiger, Tower Hill; the White Hart, Bishopsgate; and the Mitre, Hatton Garden.

But while we have nothing so ancient as the monastic inns of the country, we have still quite a number which, though not so old as the rebuilt houses just mentioned, survive in a contemporary dress old enough to be interesting. The best-known of these, of course, is the George, in Borough High Street, the last of London's galleried inns. Then Fleet Street's Cheshire Cheese. Then, similar in style to the Cheshire Cheese, comes the George and Vulture, off Cornhill; though if you would like to lift a tankard under its roof, you should do it now. I'm told that it comes down next year. In the same alley off Cornhill you will find another pleasant old place, Simpson's Bar and Tavern—not to be confused with the Simpson's of Bird-in-Hand Court, off the Poultry, nor with the Simpson's of the dinner-waggons and carvers. The Simpson's of Bird-in-Hand Court, which serves the famous two-shilling Fish Ordinary, and holds the ceremony of the Guessing of the Cheese, is also agreeably old. Lunching or taking a drink there gives you the sense of being back in the secure and prosperous eighteen-fifties, when City men had fortunes in the Funds, and villas as far out as Clapham Common and Dulwich and Stoke Newington. Just across Cheapside—in Mason's Avenue, Basinghall Street—you have the Dr. Butler's Head—a delightful old house, with a picturesque front of black oak studded with brass lanterns. The sign celebrates a court physician of James I who brewed a medicinal ale of his own. Those London houses which sold this ale exhibited a portrait of the Doctor, and the Mason's Avenue tavern is a survivor which retained the doctor's head for its sign.

In a courtyard off Bow Lane, Cheapside, is a William and Mary house of more than architectural interest. Williamson's Restaurant, in its early days, was the residence of London's Lord Mayors. It filled the office of to-day's Mansion House, and filled it fitly under the immediate shadow of St. Mary-le-Bow, with the bells of Cockaigne chiming but a yard or two from the worshipful ear. To-day it is one of the most fascinating sur-

vivals of Old London, and as good a place
for lunch as the City affords. When you're
tired of fashionable restaurants, with their
modernist rooms and their obsequious waiters,
you might find an agreeable change in lunching here, or at Dr. Butler's Head, or at
Pimm's old place in the Poultry, or at the
Fish Ordinary, under the friendly service of
the English waiter. Or you might go down
Bow Lane to the corner of Watling Street,
and try the Watling Bar and Restaurant.
This, too, is pleasant, and holds a rich patina
of association with our great-grandfathers and
their great-grandfathers. It is a late seven-
teenth-century structure, with low ceilings
and rafters. It was restored in 1901, and the
restoration, unlike much work of the kind,
really did, instead of defacing it, restore it.
Its antiquity is not made blatant. It is just
a comfortable place which happens to be old.
And at midday it is made more comfortable
by a custom which is worth all your warm-
ing-pans and chairs of great men and half-
gallon pewters which are never used. At midday, with your drink you are offered a com-
plimentary, and complementary, sandwich.

If you go down Wood Street, just opposite
Bow Lane, and look for Mitre Court, you will

find the Hole in the Wall—a house lately
rebuilt on the site of an aged parent. Even
rebuilt, it is a pleasant snuggery kind of place,
with an atmosphere of its own. Below the
centre of the court are vast cellars now used
by a firm of wine-merchants, but at one time
serving as lock-up to the Wood Street Comp-
ter. A few yards away, in Honey Lane
Market, you will find the Poulters' Arms,
another place with that atmosphere which
the eighteenth and nineteenth centuries so
valued. The sign of this house must be an
echo of the days when that section of Cheapside called the Poultry was actually the
poultry section of the West Chepe, or market.
It has two entrances, one in Freeman's Court,
the other in Trump Street, opposite the spot
once covered by a famous coaching-house—
Blossom's Inn. In Walbrook, by the Mansion
House, is an elderly place with the odd sign
of The Deacons, and Knightrider Street has
Hartridge's Horn Tavern, which looks as
though it had been well frequented by the
grandfathers of the middle-aged.

Autumn and winter are the best time for
visiting these old City places. They are for
dull days and chill nights, when the light of
their fires, glancing upon their old wood,

THE ENGLISH WAITER

makes a domestic dream of sunshine past and to come. The architects who designed them seem to have thought only of the first and last few months of the year. They assumed, I suppose, that all summer custom would drift out to the pleasure gardens at Sadler's Wells, Bagnigge Wells, the Yorkshire Stingo, Bermondsey Spa, and Ranelagh. They designed, too, not only for English winter but almost for Greenland winter. They set their places in niches of alleys, and at angles of inner courtyards, as though winter in London meant continuous nor'-easters and daily blizzards. They double-doored them, and used all their craft against that, to them, fearsome element —fresh air. So, to find them in their fullest being, you need to choose a day when the sky is hard and the wind bites through your modern hygienic underwear and your modern open-pored skin. You will then bless the ancient architect for his double doors, and the landlord for his glowing fire—or more likely, his radiator.

While you are in the City quarter, and in the tavern mood (if you can endure the City atmosphere), there are some half-dozen other places you might look at; places either actually old or of old establishment. In Martin Lane,

Cannon Street, you will find the Wine Shades, dated 1663; near it, in Crooked Lane, is the Crooked Billet, ancient but rebuilt in ancient style; and a few yards down Cannon Street, at the corner of Abchurch Lane, is the White Hart, also of ancient foundation. Then in Fenchurch Street you have the East India Arms, one of the few old buildings still left in that street; and in Billiter Street, off Fenchurch Street, is the Imperial, with delightful Victorian windows and exterior. Just such a house as Mr. Bultitude would have lunched at, in those Anstey days of hansoms and "express" omnibuses. On Tower Hill you have the Tiger, which was there in Tudor times, and stands now in modern reproduction of its old form. In Crutched Friars, you may find, under the railway arch, the Old Cheshire Cheese, which has its own style and atmosphere, and is truly old without being aged. How long it has been there I do not know, but near it is a narrow passage called French Ordinary Court, which carries a faint echo of Wycherley; and some way on its other side is a Stuart house that escaped the Great Fire.

If you go from Tower Hill along Minories, you will come out at Aldgate, and there you can pry about for the Hoop and Grapes, a house of the early eighteenth century, with contemporary windows and carved door-posts. And then, across the road, you can find an old wine-house—Webb's. And then in Bevis Marks you can find a quiet little place, the Red Lion, which pious Dickensians have identified as the house to which Dick Swiveller *might* have slipped—and perhaps slips even now—between his duties to Mr. Sampson Brass. And at the corner of Leman Street you will find another Red Lion associated with another Dick. This is a modern house, but it stands on the site of an older house, in whose yard Dick Turpin is said to have shot his partner Tom King, while aiming at the Bow Street runner who held him. Captain Johnson's *Lives of the Highwaymen* shows us that these lads of the road, who made such play with the pistol, were often, through nervousness, indifferent marksmen.

If you would like to sit in a place which is almost as it was when your great-great-grandfather last saw it, you must go to Henekey's, at High Holborn, just by Gray's Inn gateway—not upstairs, but to the long hall at the end of the ground-floor passage. There you will find a spacious, raftered chamber dressed up to the roof with huge wine and spirit casks, and in its feeling you will recognize a slowly-acquired burnish of age. You may take your drink at the bar, or in one of the many little boxes or hidey-holes which line the farther wall. Each is furnished with solid table and chairs, hat pegs, and pewter water-jug. You may read *The Times*, which stands regularly on a rack at the entrance; you may dip into the biscuit-basket; and if you wish for pen and ink, you can get them.

Another place which is much as it was in great-great-grandfather's time is the Rainbow, in Fleet Street—now a Bodega, but at one time one of the first of London's coffee-houses. And there is Stone's in Panton Street, off Haymarket; and the Coffee Pot at the corner of Warwick Lane; and the Lamb, at Lamb's Conduit Street, which I like for its cabinet photographs of the smooth-browed goddesses of the London stage of the 'eighties and 'nineties. And there is the Two Chairmen, in Bruton Mews, Mayfair, and the Talbot and the Nottingham Castle, in Little Chester Street. And there is the Windmill, at St. John Street, Clerkenwell—one of the few remaining hotels in the City region; and the Rose and Crown, whose signboard

at one time stated the democratic truth
that it was "The Only Pub in Park Lane";
and the Queen's Larder, in Queen Square,
Bloomsbury: a small place whose scrubbed
tables and wooden benches give it much the
feeling of a village inn; and a house behind
the Russell Hotel with the inviting sign of
the Friend at Hand. And on Bankside you
may find the Anchor, a delightful little place
of late seventeenth century, with secret stair-
cases and two walled-up rooms. Farther out,
you have the Flask, at Highgate; the Spani-
ards and Jack Straw's Castle, at Hampstead;
Dulwich Wood House, near the Crystal
Palace; the Doves, at Hammersmith Mall;
the Prospect of Whitby, at Wapping Wall;
the Grapes, at Limehouse; and a little Victorian place which I need hardly mention,
because I can't remember its name; but you
will find it in a street off Abbey Road, N.W.,
and it stands in a line of villas, and looks
just like one of them.

So much for the older houses—a brief
anthology which your own wanderings and
memories will permit you to amplify.

Many of the younger generation think of
London as always a vast city; yet its major

growth has happened only within the last hundred years. Up to Victoria's first decade it was little more than a large town, with the country lapping its outer streets at Lambeth, at Stepney, at Kensington, and at Marylebone. You have indications of this in the rustic note of many of our tavern signs —incongruous in the centre of a modern metropolis. In Oxford Street is the Hog in the Pound; in Piccadilly, the Yorkshire Grey; in Praed Street, the Load of Hay; in Shoe Lane, the Wheatsheaf; and in almost every quarter you find a Black Bull, a White Horse, a Bird-in-Hand, a Falcon, a Windmill, a Fox and Goose, a Green Man (forest ranger), a Plough and Harrow, a Barley Mow. You find, too, indications of our nautical interests in the Barge Aground, the Sheer Hulk, the China Ship, the Sea Serpent, the Bombay Grab, the Ship and Shovel (Sir Cloudesley), the Hearts of Oak. What you seldom find is what you would most expect to find—a full recognition of London things and of London men who have celebrated London.

True, there is the London Tavern, already mentioned, and in Farringdon Road there is a Metropolitan Tavern. But where is the John Stow's Head, the Charles Dickens' Head,

the G. A. Sala's Head? Scores of admirals
and generals are honoured, and there are
many George the Fourths, William the
Fourths, and (at Stratford Broadway) an
Edward the Seventh—the only sign I know
to that lover of life's good things. Years
ago there was a Dick Whittington, in Cloth
Fair; a Garrick's Head, in Bow Street; and
in Bolt Court a Dr. Johnson's Head. And I
admit that we still have a Ben Jonson in
Stepney; a Dean Swift off Whitechapel Road;
a Sir Richard Steele at Haverstock Hill; and
a Kemble's Head at Long Acre. But these
are a mere handful. We have no Pepys'
Head; no honour to Pierce Egan, Albert
Smith, Walter Besant, George R. Sims, or
the other London writers; no dim place in
a dim street of Bloomsbury with the sign of
the George Gissing. Surely Lamb should have
a sign, who so delighted in taverns, notably
in those nights with Coleridge at the Cat
and Salutation which stood in Newgate Street
—"that nice little smoky room, with all its
associated train of pipes, tobacco, egg-hot,
welsh-rabbits, metaphysics and poetry". Certain other tavern-lovers deserve recognition:
Boswell, for one; and Thackeray (though he
has an hotel); and Mark Lemon and the author

of *The Flying Inn*. And surely Hogarth's name would go more fitly with a public-house than with a select publishing house? There is, in Shoreditch, the London Apprentice, but I think it has nothing to do with his Industrious and Idle Apprentices. It celebrates, I fancy, the melancholy George Barnwell and his paramour, Sarah Milwood, set in scarlet by George Lillo's play:

"Am I not a wretch indeed, not only to rob my master, who placed unbounded confidence in me, but I must also murder my beloved uncle! Oh, Milwood, revoke the cruel sentence, and I will worship you for ever!"

"Away with this hypocritical whine, Barnwell. Come—there is too much time lost already—the sunbeams have risen above the window. Here is brandy—drink deep!— again, and yet again!"

Magog, Falstaff, Nell Gwynne, and the Blind Beggar of Bethnal Green are set on London sign-boards, but these are figures of London legend rather than its celebrants. And if Falstaff is to be recognized, why not creations of the fancy who were more closely concerned with London? Surely the Borough High Street should have a Weller's Head, and Goswell Road a Pickwick Arms? The rubicund head of John Jorrocks would give a desired bit of colour to Coram Street, and Tooley Street certainly should recognize those Three Tailors. Somewhere off Commercial Road there is a Grundy Arms, but it does not, I think, celebrate that unseen character of Morton's play who has become a figure of common allusion. Perhaps she would hardly attract custom, though another of Morton's characters, also a household word, would grace any tavern with his name; we would all be gratified in taking a drink at the sign of Sir Hubert Stanley. Some Kennington tavern might well celebrate its most famous son and the most famous of all Cockneys with the Chaplin's Head; and any tavern around Baker Street would double its custom under the sign of the Sherlock Holmes.

Of abstruse signs London can show almost as many as the countryside, especially in corners of original London—the City, South London, and the East. In Bermondsey you will find the Lilliput Hall and, most aptly, the Simon the Tanner; and at Rotherhithe the Old China Hall. In Wardour Street is the Intrepid Fox, which is not, as you might think, an echo of the chase; it is an echo of Charles James. Gray's Inn Road has the Mechanic's Larder; Wood Street, the Bell and Bird Cage; and South Kensington the Hoop and Toy. Upper East Smithfield gives you the New York Stores (I wonder why); and in other parts of the East you will find the Salmon and Ball, the Blade Bone, the Silver Trumpet, the Refiner's Arms, the Grave Maurice, the Widow's Son, the Bombay Grab (near Bow Bridge), the Coal-Meter's Arms; and on the Isle of Dogs, as heaven is my judge, you will find in West Ferry Road a house with the sign of the Magnet and Dewdrop. The East End affords also signs of a genial quality suited to the tavern and all that it means: the Old Friends, the Golden Heart, the Darby and Joan, the Horn of Plenty. With signs of this note to be chosen, and with many historic London characters who might be celebrated, I wonder why two houses—one in Whitechapel Road, and one in a street off Edgware Road—chose for their signs such distressing reminders, respectively, as the London Hospital Tavern and the Rent Day.

The club that we know to-day in Pall Mall and St. James developed from the coteries of the coffee-houses and taverns of the late eighteenth century. But the tavern-club is not wholly supplanted, and the modern tavern still nurses many a fraternity. In some suburban districts it serves as the Masonic Lodge of that district, and in more homely parts it is the local headquarters for such friendly societies as the Buffaloes, the Druids, and the Oddfellows. In Central London the larger tavern-restaurants serve, as in Johnson's time, as the centres of various dining-clubs. The Cheshire Cheese and Anderton's, for example, are, or have been, the rendezvous of a score or more groups and clubs. To men of letters the most interesting of these was the Rhymers' Club of the 'nineties, which met at the Cheshire Cheese, and had among its members Lionel Johnson, Ernest Dowson, Arthur Symons and Le Gallienne. It is now part of literary history, and the two little volumes of verse which it issued have what booksellers call rarity value. It was followed some years later by the Songsters. Neither, I believe, lived very long. London's taverns and cafés of the latter age have not been of a kind in which a practising poetic coterie can flourish. But they are of a kind in which pious groups, bound to a common point of interest or study, can meet and dine and talk. The George and Vulture is still the rendezvous of the City Pickwick Club; a Dr. Johnson Club holds an annual dinner at the Cheshire Cheese; and London's oldest debating society—Ye Antient Society of Cogers—after many changes of rendezvous meets at the Cannon, in Cannon Street.

In a book on London restaurants, published in the 'nineties, the author, Edmund Callow, mentions a Cheshire Cheese dining-club which called itself, in that facetiousness which at times overcomes the Englishman—the Kernoozers. This was a puzzle to most of those who heard of it. Even when they learned that all the members were collectors, it remained a puzzle unless they recalled the French word for the expert in taste. In and about London you may find a hundred of these whimsical clubs or groups attached to taverns. In recent years, the most widely known was the Froth-Blowers, which had branches in all London districts and throughout the country. Facetious in its name and in its rules, its purpose was sober enough— the raising of funds for the treatment of crippled children. Among the members of

its various lodges, or Vats, were numbers of
men of serious position and habit; men whom
a foreigner, unaware of the inwardness of
the frozen Englishman, could never imagine
in the rôle of Froth-Blower, singing the
Froth-Blower's Anthem—"The more we are
together, together, together . . ."

To the man who never enters a bar, all
bars are alike. But each has its difference—
difference in atmosphere (which derives from
the personality of the landlord), difference in
company, and difference in little touches for
comfort; or the absence of them. There are
many taverns which, while not housing any
club, are a centre for a group which makes
it, for a time, its meeting-place, and gives
it distinction and character. A comfortable
little bar in Poppin's Court, off Fleet Street,
received from a gossip-writer, in the nineteen-
twenties, the name of the Poets' Corner. It
stood near the office of one of the literary
monthlies, whose editor and staff found it
convenient for a midday drink and sandwich.
Around them gathered the contributors and
the would-be contributors, and as most of
these were recognized poets, or had published
the usual "slim volume", the name stuck.
Some few years ago Mr. Eric Linklater gave

a title to one of his novels—Poet's Pub—
which caused raised eyebrows in circles unaware of the long association of the poet and
the pub. The association, of course, goes
back to the Mermaid and the Devil, and runs
through English poetry up to last week. It
would be indiscreet to say anything about
last week, but many poets, lately gone, have
been seen, by those now living, meditating
upon their art at tavern boards, and gathering groups around them. In the recent past
there was the type that remained faithful to
the Café Royal; and there was the type that
preferred the common London bar. Stephen
Phillips was a respected visitor to the little
wine-bar at the bottom of Villiers Street.
Ernest Dowson, before spending his mid-
nights in cabmen's shelters, was to be seen
at the Cock, in Shaftesbury Avenue, or the
Crown, at the corner of Cranbourn Street
and Charing Cross Road. Swinburne, every
day for many years, took his morning draught
at the house on Putney Heath—was it the
Green Man? And within my own time, if
you wanted to listen to acidly amusing talk,
you could go to the Wheatsheaf, in Shoe
Lane, between six and seven, and sit with
T. W. H. Crosland, whose *Collected Poems*

FAITHFUL TO THE CAFÉ ROYAL

betray a true poet known to the general public only as a journalist.

The "group" note is found in almost all bars save those at railway stations. Around Hatton Garden the note is gems; down-stream, in the docks district, it is river and sea; in the bars of Euston Road and Great Portland Street, it is cars; and in the bars of Mayfair and that part of Belgravia off Grosvenor Place, you will find grave, upright men who look like stage dukes and are real-life butlers, footmen, and private chauffeurs. At the Pakenham Arms, a nice old place at Knightsbridge Green, by Tattersall's, you find men in riding cords and hard grey hats, faithful in an age of petrol to the horse. If, in the modern morbid concern with health, you wanted to know the latest thing in surgical operations, you could satisfy your curiosity at the Ship and Shovel in St. Thomas Street, by listening to the students of Guy's; or at the little bar in Gower Place frequented by those in training at Gower Street. In the bars around Smithfield you are in a company of straw hats and fat-stock prices, and in Long Acre you will hear about bananas green or "turning", and the shortage of lemons.

If you like the company of artists, you

will find it at the Six Bells and the Cadogan, in King's Road, Chelsea; or at the Fitzroy, in Charlotte Street, and the Swiss Cottage, St. John's Wood. Actors are not now seen so commonly in bars as they were in the distant days when they wore coats with astrakhan collars, and had all played Second Murderer to the Old Man's Macbeth. But Rule's, in Maiden Lane, still keeps the theatre note. So does the Bedford Head, in that lane, and its rehearsal rooms are in constant use. In the astrakhan days, the Bedford Street Bodega, with its priceless cheese (it was free to all), buzzed with theatrical talk; indeed, all the bars of the Strand and its by-streets held this talk, and were filled with dark and stately figures who could not order a glass of your best bitter and a welsh rabbit without the air of plucking from the memory a rooted sorrow. This pseudo-romantic atmosphere and all the "mystery" of the theatre craft has now been blown upon; and your modern actor, old or young, famous or obscure, would pass anywhere as a man about town or a bank clerk. But the old school, with its air of withdrawal in a high and sacred voca-tion, had its quality. At least, it made the Bedford Street Bodega a centre of a period,

DARK AND STATELY FIGURES

as Will's Coffee House, and Button's, were
centres of their period. In the 'nineties, all
stories of hard-up or faded actors were set at
this Bodega, and when I was in my teens such
stories were a sort of currency of anecdote.

There was the story of the-man-who-had-
played-with-Irving sitting in the Bodega and
looking sadly at the lees of his glass, which
nobody was offering to refill. To him came
a stranger. "Pardon me, but they're short
of change here. D'you happen to have change
for a sovereign?" "I have not, sir. None the
less, sir"—raising hat—"I thank you for the
compliment." And the old actor, deploring,
in the manner of the middle-aged, the changed
times. "No, sir; all the old amenities are
gone. Vanished with the rose. The old man-
ners, the old courtesy, the old graces that
made life sweet. All is hurry and selfishness
and thick skin. Only this morning, for example, I went into the Bodega to get a cigar.
Some clumsy fool trod on me fingers, and
never even said Sorry." And another old
actor meeting a fellow-actor in the Strand,
who inquires what he's doing. "Resting,
laddie. Resting, for a period." "Splendid.
Splendid. Lunching anywhere particular to-
day?" "No; just lunching at the Cheese."

"Ha—the Cheshire Cheese—the pudding—eh?" "No, you fool—the one in Bedford Street." The Bodega had two entrances—one at either end of its frontage. In the years before the War I was there one evening when a played-with-Irving type sauntered in. He scanned the bar and each table for a possible host, sauntered the length of the room with roving and unrewarded eye, and passed out by the other door. I remarked to the manager: "He didn't spend much." The manager said: "No. We have a lot of them here. I call them my Arcade Customers."

There is one actor story which might be called the story that disposes for ever of all actor stories. It is the story of the old actor of the Bodega school seeking lodgings in South London. At a house exhibiting a card, he knocked. "I see that you have—ah—lodgings to let."

"That's right."

"Can you—ah—give me your lowest terms for actorrs?"

"Yes, I can. A pack of lazy ——, ——, ——, ——, ——. Good night."

In the days when music-hall was flourishing it was a separate world from that of the theatre, and its members had their own resorts. One of these was the house at the corner of York Road, over Waterloo Bridge, where the agents then had their offices. Another was Yates' Wine Lodge, in the Strand, which had the old Tivoli facing it. And as most of them lived in South London, they had a Sunday morning rendezvous at the White Horse, Brixton, where many of them trifled only with lime-juice or lemonade. Now that the music-hall artiste, as a special type, is fading from the scene, there is no house with the purely music-hall note. The new form of entertainer is the radio artiste, and since radio is modern, its company has a modern meeting-place. At a bright restaurant and bar, the Bolivar, just behind the Langham Hotel and but a few yards from Broadcasting House, you may see from time to time most of those whose names are indeed household words; those who hope that their names may some day be household words; and those who like to mix with and use the Christian names of those whose surnames are household words.

The group note is to be found too in bars of national colour, and if you wish to see nationalism in ardent expression, you need not go so far as Italy or Germany. You need

only go to one of the Irish houses—Ward's
or Mooney's—on St. Patrick's Night; or one
of the Scotch Houses—Milford Lane, Cranbourn Street, or Cambridge Circus—on St.
Andrew's Night. Where the Welsh let off
their nationalism on St. David's Night, I
don't know. Possibly as kings of the dairy
trade they do it in one of the new Milk Bars.
The Scotch Stores in Cranbourn Street, by
the way, is kept by a comedian, Mr. Jimmy
Russell, who, many years ago, was the bun-
throwing schoolboy in that historic sketch of
Fred Karno's, "Mumming Birds". He played
opposite a then unknown comedian named
Charles Chaplin.

Around Aldgate, Whitechapel and Spital-
fields, of course, the note is markedly Jewish.
A few bars in this district have Jewish landlords, and the strong family sense of this
race is reflected in the bar. They have not
the coming-and-going busy-ness of the ordinary London bar, but rather the air of the
Continental café. Everybody seems to know
everybody, and everybody talks. There is
not only the fact of family—the attendants
are usually sons and daughters or grandsons
of the landlord; there is a distinct feeling of
family among the customers, down to remote

IN THESE INDIVIDUAL BARS THE TALK HAS ONE
DEFINED NOTE

cousinship. A feeling of a nice family, I
should add, remembering the retort of the
actress to the gossip-writer who said that the
company of the So-and-So Theatre was like
one large family: "It's a lie. We get on
awfully well together." Everybody in these
Jewish bars, on either side of the counter,
gets on well together; and if the baby-carriage
is in everybody's way, and each newcomer
stumbles over the grandchild's rocking-horse,
nobody complains. The presence of these
domestic items is considered as much a part
of that particular bar's furniture, as its
bottles and glasses, and its counter-decora-
tion of strange sausages, pickles, and potato-
cakes. These things are a feature of every
Jewish bar, where food seems to be held as
something one takes between meals. The
walls are usually decorated with posters in
Hebrew, announcing meetings of the many
friendly societies; and posters in English
announcing those boxing events in which,
as in dance-bands, the Jewish race is so
prominent.

In all these individual bars the talk has
one defined note, according to the group
which has staked a claim on that bar. But
when shop-talk is done, then the talk in all

bars is much the same. Women, I believe, often wonder what men talk about when no women are present. Many of them, I fancy, have the notion that the talk is concerned with woman and with unprintable stories. It isn't. A woman might eavesdrop for three months in poor pubs and rich clubs, and scarcely hear woman mentioned. The chief topic among men is Money. Then Sport. Then—a long way down—Politics. And then, very largely, Trivia. But Money first. Woman likes spending money. Man likes making it. Always it is his first subject, and only when he has no more to say about it does he turn to other things, such as Sport and Trivia.

The Trivia talk is perhaps the most amusing to the outside listener. Every evening, in London bars as in village inns, you may hear profound debates, and solemn quotation of authorities, on points of no more consequence than your last week's breakfasts. Statement, denial, argument, rejoinder, pass and re-pass on such trifles as the smallest county in England. ("Rutland." "No, the County of London." "Let's get a map.") Or on when the Derby was run in a snowstorm. Or what Gladstone really did say in 1882. Or when

Disraeli first took office as Prime Minister.
("He never did." "Don't talk nonsense."
"He never did. There's no such office as
Prime Minister." "Oh? What about Ten
Downing Street? Isn't that the residence of
the Prime Minister?" "No. It's the residence
of the First Lord of the Treasury.") That is
why good landlords always keep a copy of
Whittaker's, Pears', Wisden's and Ruff's
Guide. They know that men will deal more
tractably with the urgent question of "Time,
Gentlemen!" when they have settled the more
urgent questions of what quarter of London
saw the first mechanical tram-car; how many
Cabinet portfolios Mr. Winston Churchill has
carried; and the exact figure of Walter
Lindrum's biggest break.

This idle and amiable argument has been
a feature of tavern life since there were
taverns, as you may see from the tavern
scenes of Shakespeare and Ben Jonson. It '
keeps the company sweet and maintains the
true tavern atmosphere, which is geniality.
You may, here and there in taverns, see a
gloomy man drinking gloomily and alone, in
the vain hope of drowning a gloom that has
learned to swim; but the regular note is
geniality. That is why charity collectors

always make a tour of the bars, and why
hawkers, if the landlord permits, can get rid
of almost anything, even to tortoises. The
Salvation Army paper, the *War Cry*, is
regularly offered in certain bars on Friday
nights; indeed, only in bars have I seen it
offered. Any knowledgeable wife, noting, on
a Friday night, a copy of the *War Cry* mixed
up with her husband's evening paper, can
instantly guess where he loitered on the way
home.

In many a bar the landlord's geniality
spatters out into facetiousness, in the form
of notices or announcements. Fun or facetiousness is seldom found in your draper's,
bootmaker's, hatter's or tailor's; only your
tavern landlord makes a jest of his business;
and by the cards and decorations of his bar
you may guess his character. Most of those
who have ever entered a bar are familiar
with the card reading: WYBADIITY; and most
of us have at some time "bought it". It
evokes the obvious question:"What's the
meaning of that?" To which the barman
answers: "Will you buy a drink if I tell you?"
And you say "Yes"; and he says he'll have
a dry ginger. And if you claim that he hasn't
yet told you, he urges you to have another

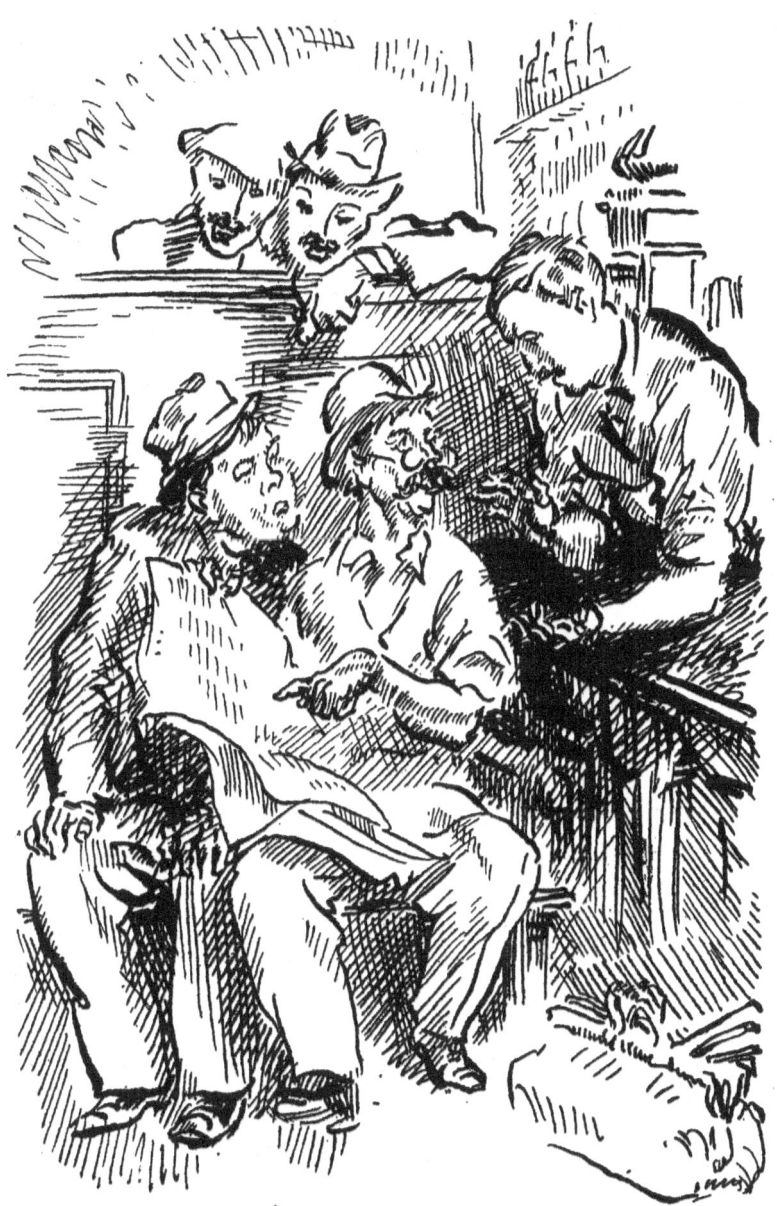

THIS IDLE AND AMIABLE ARGUMENT HAS BEEN A
FEATURE OF TAVERN LIFE

look at the card. And then there's the
"A B C D gold-fish" catch. And the "You
May Telephone From Here. And Tell Her
You're Kept At The Office." And a new note,
which I found in a Soho bar. The usual door
labelled "Gentlemen" bore an additional line:
"This May Not Apply To You, But It's The
Place You're Looking For." Sometimes, in
bringing the law to the notice of customers,
the cards give fine, confused reading. For
example: "Betting and Gambling, on Becoming Known to the Proprietor, Will be Prose-
cuted"—which evokes a Pilgrim's Progress
scene of the appearance in court of Mr.
Betting and Mr. Gambling. While a Bloomsbury tavern claims a monopoly of tavern
business with "No Drinking Allowed Outside
These Premises". During the War, when the
No-Treating regulation was in force, one saw
many an oblique effort at bringing this to
plain language. Thus: "Each Customer Must
Pay For Their Own Drink"; and "Customers
are Warned that You Cannot Pay for Your
Friend's Drink": and my favourite bit of
crewel-work in English: "Each Customer Take
Notice That They Must Call and Pay Seperate
For Your Own." And there was one which
may have been conceived in error, and was

preserved with a private grin: "No Treating
Aloud".

None but a man of genial temper can keep
a tavern or an inn. It is a job that calls
for patience, tact, understanding, wide interests (or sincere assumption of them) and that
love of mankind in its bright or sorry aspects
which these qualities imply. The good landlord, indeed, must be, as the schoolboy said
of Cæsar's wife, all things to all men; and if,
as I suggested, those of the past would find
the modern tavern the same in atmosphere
as those that they knew, so, if a landlord
of the past met a landlord of these days, he
would recognize some quiddity akin to his
own. Chaucer's description of Henry Bailey
of the Tabard fits equally the good landlord
of these times; and Dame Quickly, of the
Boar's Head, is still with us. So is Wagstaff,
of the Half-Moon, in Little Britain; and while
we have happily rid ourselves of Eleanour
Rummyng, we have to-day many a landlady
as bright and kind as Bess Bridges of Hey-
wood's Fair Maid of the West. A man of
mean outlook may keep various kinds of
shop, and keep them successfully to his profit;
such a man behind a bar would be in the

Gazette within a year. For the bar, as I have said, is the place where a man chooses to be himself, and the landlord must conspire to help him to it; acknowledging his whims, and agreeing with his views; or, when disagreeing, doing so in a man-to-man way that leads the customer to admire his own arguments. As, in another sphere, the *maître d'hôtel* must be a model of politesse and suavity —which in his case sometimes degenerates into slaver—so your good landlord must be a model of easy-going good-fellowship, never aloof and never unctuous.

Centuries ago, John Earle defined the bar as the busy man's recreation, the melancholy man's sanctuary, the stranger's welcome, the scholar's kindness, and the citizen's courtesy. To keep such a place, where all men's angles may find their niche, is a task for a man of parts, a true husbandman and householder. He must, in a large way, perform the office of the ordinary family man, and must find his life's pleasure in performing it. He must maintain a domestic atmosphere orderly but free, and must see that all members of the family are happy, neither spoiling one nor neglecting another. He must know something of everything, and so talk business with the commercial man, sport with the plus-fours man, crime with the morbid man, high finance with the stockbroker's clerk, and the shortcomings of the local Council with fellow-tradesmen. He must commiserate the man who has flung out from a discordant domestic atmosphere, and rejoice with the man who has drawn the winner in the office sweep. His business is a craft, but he must be more than a craftsman. The successful and popular landlord needs to be something of an artist and much of a psychologist. His position is genially conveyed by the sign of a house in Marylebone High Street—the Shepherd and Flock—which, if it implies that customers are sheep, carries the assurance that they are in good hands.

But while landlords are true exemplars of tradition, one cannot hold the same of the quality of some of their refreshments. Nobody of these times wants or could take strong liquor, but could we not have lightness without the laboratory? "Home-brewed" may still be found in certain country towns, but I know of no London house that offers it. Machine production of food and drink, like machine production of other things, gives us something slick and sterile; hygienic methods,

WHERE ALL MEN'S ANGLES MAY FIND THEIR NICHE

admirable though they are, remove not only imperfections, but virtues. In all crafts, whether the making of wine or beer, the making of clothes, the making of furniture or bread or pastry, you must, for vitality and character, have the touch of the living human hand. And in all departments of our daily needs, the touch of the human hand has been, or is being, obliterated—often on the plea that the human hand is insanitary. It may be; but I doubt that the human hand in its most soiled condition could produce less agreeable food or furniture than that produced by some hygienic machines. The man who held that there was no such thing as bad liquor—it was only that some was better than others—should have lived to taste some of the concoctions offered in these days. He might then wonder whether certain vintners ever could, even on the nether floor of a bargain basement, buy anything half so horrid as the goods they sell.

You have heard, perhaps, the story of the complaining customer and the protesting landlord? Against the customer's complaint of the quality of the beer (which he said was as tart as a school-mistress the morning after Parents' Day) the landlord held that the beer he supplied had given satisfaction to his customers for twenty years, and was the best to be had. If the customer still doubted, the landlord would give him a sample which he could take to the Public Analyst, and then he'd see. The customer took the sample and carried it to the Town Hall. But at the Town Hall it went astray and got into the department of the Officer of Health, and the customer got it back with a report that the drains of that house must be seen to at once. What the report would be on some of the synthetic drinks that are now becoming so popular, is matter for contemplation on wet Wednesdays.

Speaking of wine—I mean real wine—a welcome addition to the London scene would be a group of wine-bars which covered the whole wine-list. The majority of wine-bars seem to limit themselves to sherry, port, madeira and champagne. At only a few special places can one call for a little Niersteiner or Zeltinger, a glass of a good Bordeaux, or Chianti or Capri. The wines of France and Germany of course present the difficulty that a bottle once opened is useless next day; but surely, where demand is not constant, this could be covered by stocking

the quarter-bottles which are common in
Europe. Still, if we cannot everywhere get
draughts of the lighter wines of Europe, we
can get the apparently light but often potent
wines of the West of England. We have
to-day no Cyder Cellars, with a singer to
scare the skin off us with the ballad of Sam
Hall, but we have Cyder Stores, where that
drink, with perry, makes the main business.
One of these is in London Road, near St.
George's Circus, and another at the Edgware
Road end of Harrow Road. There may be
others.

In recent years we have heard much of
the "improved" tavern, and in and about
London some twenty examples are before us.
These have yet to work (or play) themselves
into the social scene. For the moment they
have the air of having been just unpacked,
which taverns should not have. All taverns
must at some time be new, but, as with
human creatures, their youth is merely a
probation period. With the passing of time,
no doubt, these new taverns, by long association with men, will mellow and acquire the
necessary glaze. Their tables and chairs will
grow with the rubbings of the years, and

their oak frames and window glass will become richer by stress and weather. Anyway,
even in their temporary newness, they certainly are a welcome replacement of the
dingy, penitential bars of the later nineteenth
century, which survive here and there in the
suburbs and around the railway termini. It
was such places, I think, that brought upon
the tavern its bad name and the social slur
involved in visiting it. After a glance and a
smell at these relics, one can sympathize
with the people who saw the tavern as an
abomination. Indeed, the very style of them
suggests that their owners and builders also
saw the tavern as an abomination and resolved
to make it so. The shabby-flash front, the
grime and dull glitter of the interior, the
dock-like compartments which screened the
customer in one bar from customers in other
bars, and even screened him, by an erection
of movable glass shutters, from the staff, and
almost made him, when asked for his order,
plead Guilty—these things gave the aboli-
tionists a powerful weapon. If the American
abolitionist, Carrie Nation, when she came to
London thirty years ago, had employed her
axe on such places, or her successor, Mr. Johnson, had directed his disgust at them instead

SCREENED BY MOVABLE GLASS SHUTTERS

of at good drinks, all men, whether teetotallers or taverners, would have applauded.

Still, those that remain are going one by one, and in place of the gin-palace we have the bright, wide-windowed, airy tavern-restaurant, with mural decorations by real artists. One could wish, though, that the designs were more of these times. Tavern architecture seemed to come to a stop in the eighteen-twenties, and has never since found a new step. With all the new ideas and forms in building that Germany and America and Scandinavia have given us, tavern architects seem unable to do more than hark back to the external forms of Tudor or Queen Anne or the early Georges. Maybe this is intentional. Maybe they work on the assumption that the tavern man is linked with tradition, and has an antiquarian streak; and in default of genuine Jacobean will prefer the reproduction to the steel and concrete of to-day. None the less, this is wrong. Everything newly made should be of its age. Those Georgian taverns of 1740 which we now cherish, were built as Georgian taverns, not as replicas of Elizabethan models. They were proud in being the latest thing and in using the latest ideas in domestic architecture, and our taverns of to-day should be as original as the old once were. The interiors of the new places certainly are adapted to modern times, and this makes it the more puzzling that the outer design should cling to gables and "black-and-white" work, or the red brick and flat façades of the Georges.

These interiors, and their general appointments, would give a wanderer from the 'seventies the shock of coming suddenly from gloom to sun. They are arranged to encourage an atmosphere in which the family can meet. Wherever possible, the new tavern has a garden for the children; or, failing that, a separate room in which the lighter drinks are served. The one bar is open to full view, and the main furniture is not bevelled mirrors frosted with brewers' advertisements, but tables and chairs. Flowers are freely used; not paper daffodils or celluloid poppies, but flowers. Illustrated papers are supplied, and all the necessary materials for board games; and a snack bar is an important and popular feature. In short, it is what the tavern should be and, until the late nineteenth century, was—a temporary home.

Games, indoor and outdoor, have been a feature of tavern life ever since taverns arrived. The earliest was obviously that game which is commemorated on so many signboards—Chequers—a form of draughts. Skittles indoors and bowls outdoors were also played in the earliest times; and there was a game called variously shovel-board or shuffle-board. Walton has it in *The Compleat Angler*—"I have caught but five trouts; for indeed we went to a good honest ale-house, and there we played at shovel-board half the day." And Pepys knew it—"It being very warm and pleasant, to Bowe, and thence to Hackney. There light, and played at shuffle-board." Chess, dominoes, quoits and bagatelle were common in the past, and up to the nineteenth century every kind of card and dice gaming was usual: Primero, Hazard, Spanish Triumph, Blind Hookey. To-day, the most common games are billiards (where they have a room), darts, shove-halfpenny, and the American pin-table. In Central London the pin-table seems to have swept the others away; but dart-teams may be found along the river and in the suburbs, and occasionally shove-halfpenny, which is seen in almost all village inns. I lately saw shove-halfpenny being played in a bar twenty paces from Old Bond Street. Until last year, when

I stopped at a Hampshire inn, I had not known that it was a recognized game, with a supervising body and written laws. But at this inn I happened to pick up the "half-pennies"—discs of white metal—and found them engraved as having been approved by "The Shove-Halfpenny Control Association". The old game of Bumble-Puppy may still be played at that pleasant eighteenth-century riverside inn, the Doves, at Hammersmith, where Thomson wrote one of the books of his Seasons, and where to-day a literary company still gathers. Bowls may be played at the Six Bells, Chelsea, and at many suburban houses; and the Red Lion, at Hammersmith Mall, has a skittle-alley and a team of which Mr. A. P. Herbert was captain; and I hope still is, despite the cares of parliament.

With the spread of mass-entertainment and mechanical amusements, many of the tavern's amenities of the past have fallen into disuse. Mumming and puppet-shows went long ago, but the glee-party and the sing-song, common in the Tudor and Stuart times, survived into the nineteenth century. Pepys attended many a glee-party in taverns, and you remember that sing-song in *The Compleat Angler*, when Coridon, Piscator, Peter and Venator took

SHOVE-HALFPENNY

turns at country songs; and that Three Pigeons sing-song in *She Stoops to Conquer*. Indeed, wherever you get a tavern scene in the old novelists and dramatists, you almost certainly get a sing-song. In the past this amusement could be spontaneous anywhere; to-day it is an offence unless the landlord holds a music licence. If the fine weather, or a stroke of good fortune, or a sudden apprehension that life is sweet, impels you to burst into song in a tavern, you will first be looked at as though mad, or drunk; and then you will swiftly be suppressed. The only permitted singing means an organized affair in a special room with a dais and a music-licence; though, if you have the nerve, you can get round this. Though you may not sing *in* the tavern you may sing just outside it. You may carry your banjo along to the tavern, and then you may thrust your foot inside the door, and through the crevice you may bawl or croon as many songs as you know; and then you may go round the bar with your offertory bag. The law makes no objection to that—which is work. It only objects to your being cheerful in the bar without filling up a form announcing that on a given date you are going to be cheerful.

But with all the mass-entertainment, and the restriction of sudden song, men in taverns seem able still to make their own amusement for their idle minutes. This is shown in those many tricks and catches which are worked only in taverns. There is the game of cork-snatching. Five men get a cork each, and set them on the table. For success, there must be four knowledgeable men and one innocent. The game is—that the man whose cork is last off the table on the word "Snatch!" pays for the company's drinks. On the word "Snatch!" of course, the innocent snatches his cork. The others do not touch theirs. As his was the last cork to be taken from the table, the privilege of paying falls to him. Then there is the game (supposedly a game of chance) of Show Most, Take All, and Pay For Drinks. Four or five men agree to show all the money in the right-hand trousers-pocket. The man who shows most takes all that the others show, and pays for their drinks. Those who know the game have already removed their silver to another pocket. The innocent brings out a handful of silver and copper; the others bring out twopence each. He takes their twopences and is allowed to spend three or four shillings for his prowess in Showing Most. In summer, there is the sugar-and-fly catch. Each man is supplied with a lump of sugar, and the man on whose sugar a fly first settles pays forfeit in a round of drinks. This, of course, is pure chance—or would be if those who know it did not first bring their sugar into contact with cigarette ash. Then there are some dozen tricks with matches which always bemuse the innocent. And the rather unfriendly trick of Carrying the Chair. The innocent is wagered a drink that he cannot carry a certain chair from the bar round the room, following each of the three walls, and not stopping on the way. He picks up the chair; finds it no heavier than any other chair; and marches with it alongside each of the three walls and back to the bar. "There you are. How's that? I claim a Bass." "Yes, you've won. There's your drink. You've earned it. If you knew what a —— fool you looked carrying that silly chair round the room!"

During last century various taverns in and around London invented little pastimes in the way of rituals and observances, or devised peculiar points of interest for the attraction and amusement of customers. At the High-

1

gate taverns there was the mock-solemn ceremony of Swearing on the Horns, with its
rigmarole exhortation beginning "Upstanding
and uncovered . . ." One or two of the Highgate houses have preserved their horns—a set
of antlers mounted on a pole. The Garrick's
Head in Bow Street had its Judge and Jury
trials. At the Widow's Son, Bromley-by-
Bow, there was the Good Friday ceremony
of distribution of hot-cross buns, and the
adding of a bun to the stack hanging from
the ceiling—a stack begun by a former landlady, whose sailor son was expected home
one Good Friday and was wrecked on the
way. A house in Catherine Street, Covent
Garden, which had an oyster counter, drew
"all London" for some time with its whistling
oyster. And a house in the obliterated Wych
Street attracted custom by its landlord's
length—which, according to Edmund Callow,
whom I quoted earlier, was seven feet six
inches. When London and its visitors had
tired of looking him up and down, he still
drew a crowd to his house: he dressed his
barmaids in the then new and daring bloomers.

Other houses invited custom by forming
collections of museum material—stuffed birds,
or perhaps an aviary of live foreign birds,

such as the George, in George Court, Strand, used to show; old armour and weapons; fossils; insects; or general curiosities. At many taverns of the near suburbs you may still see some such display; and Rule's, in Maiden Lane, still keeps, I suppose, its large collection of old playbills. One of the many touches which held Americans to the Cheshire Cheese, was the free supply of churchwarden pipes. I am told that this has now ceased, since the manufacture of these pipes is passing out; but I believe they are still supplied for group-dinners. Simpson's Fish Lunch maintains to-day its Guessing of the Cheese, already mentioned, with free champagne to the whole company in the rare event of some customer getting measurements and weight correct. The only other chance I know of a stranger getting anything free is at one of those occasions which the trade calls Change-Overs, when the incoming landlord, taking you for a possibly regular customer, asks you to join him, and the outgoing landlord, mistaking you in the rush for one of his old customers, offers a stirrup-cup.

A useful amusement for our idle minutes was invented some years ago by an anonymous student of psychology who had us well docketed for the babies that most of us are. The purpose of the amusement was to raise funds for local hospitals, and it must have raised goodly sums. The method devised by the student of our weaker moments was this. . . . The landlord kept a stock of pieces of gummed paper of many colours. You took one of these, twisted a penny into it, damped the outer surface, and flipped it to the ceiling, where it stuck. Pleased with your skill, and the pretty colours of the papers, you did it again and again, until your pennies were exhausted. Then, perhaps, pleased with your colour pattern, and anxious to develop it, you changed a shilling with the landlord (if you were from the South) and went on doing it. The ceiling of many a bar, about that time, presented a heaven of coloured stars as rich as the ceiling of that Globe tavern to which Henry Vaughan, nearly three hundred years ago, wrote his Rhapsodis.

Painted ceilings are not as common in taverns or any other houses as they were: in these days neither tavern customers nor private householders finish their evenings prone on the floor. But decoration of some sort every tavern has, and one can find much

DECORATION OF SOME SORT EVERY TAVERN HAS

private amusement in the study of it, or the attempts at it. One can, indeed, from the bars of London and their decoration, touch social history from the first George, through the eighteenth century, the three phases of Victorianism and *l'art nouveau* period, to the nineteen-twenties. Sometimes (not often) one finds a manager or landlord of an old house who actually knows its history and its main period, and is sufficiently interested to give it the apt decoration. But usually one sees contemporary Hogarth prints on the walls of a gilt-and-mirror bar of the eighteen-eighties, and on the walls of a house of 1780, crude coloured prints of motoring mishaps. If you ask why they are there, nobody can tell you. I know one landlord who has decorated his bar with steel engravings of the less-inspired works of Landseer and Marcus Stone; and the effect is wholly right. His house is of the 'forties, and he had taste enough to see that his rooms asked for just that kind of decoration. Near it is another bar with steel chairs and tables, wireless set, pin-tables, and cocktail list; and on its walls a series of Greuze plates in bird's-eye maple. Elsewhere I have seen Rowlandson prints shouting from a William Morris wallpaper; and carbon prints of Burne-Jones on the wooden walls of an old waterside tavern where the Rowlandson prints would have been in their sympathetic air.

Some London bars which have moved with the moving times seem to have grown tired at a particular period, and to have moved no more. In Central London and the near suburbs you may find many a bar which grew up to the Diamond Jubilee, and then decided to call it a career. Furniture, atmosphere and decorations are as they were in the blessed year 1897. Even the cigar-smoke of Jubilee celebrants seems to be hanging about. There you will find prints of Gladstone, of General Gordon, of Sir Garnet Wolseley, and engravings of Stanley "presuming" that he sees Dr. Livingstone before him. You will find walnut what-nots (whatever they were not, nobody seems to know what they *were*) and corner brackets in the best curly-wriggly style of the 'nineties. Any novelist contemplating a novel set around the Diamond Jubilee Year would find in these places his period, almost his world, preserved under a glass case in full breath and rumour.

The famous Long Bar of the Criterion went some years ago, but another long bar survives at the buffet of the Holborn Restaurant, and evokes a social epoch. I believe the idea of long bars was borrowed from the New York of the 'eighties. Another epoch is evoked by those giant places in the suburbs which seem, by their four or five storeys, to have been built in a sanguine mood as hotels. In their bars you may re-create the 'seventies, helped by the Empty Chair—Gad's Hill; a group picture of the Berlin Congress; a billiards table which Herbert Spencer might have cursed; a prodigal use of mahogany and gilt cornices; and the hollow upstairs rooms by which the 'seventies learned what we all know to-day—that prosperity is hiding round the other corner. A flavour, if no more, of the Tom and Jerry period may be caught in the downstairs rooms of Dirty Dick's, in Bishopsgate. The front and upper part were rebuilt some time in the 'seventies, but the lower rooms are much the kind of place to which Corinthian Tom carried his cousin. Stevens' Wine Bar, also in Bishopsgate, is another echo of this period. A good type of late seventeenth- and early eighteenth-century house is Williamson's, off Bow Lane, already mentioned; and for middle eighteenth century there are the Hoop and Grapes, at

Aldgate, and the Doves at Hammersmith. Late eighteenth you may find at Hampstead and Highgate; and the middle nineteenth you can pick up repeatedly in the City and West, and can almost identify among their customers Trollope's Charley Tudor and Surtees' Mr. Sponge. For that period which just now cannot reach our ears by direct sound, and is not at the right distance for echo—the years just before 1914—you must go to the taverns of those suburbs which at that time were new and on the edge, and now are faded and within motor-bus routes. Or you might catch it at one of the brass-and-marble places which arose around Piccadilly Circus and Leicester Square in the first decade of the century; places that had Pink Roumanian Orchestras and Blue Hungarian Bands, whose members hadn't learned that music consists in Hotcha and Boop-a-Doop.

Every tavern, as I have said, has its peculiar note and character, as every home has, even those little homes furnished on credit from mass-production stores; and the amateur of taverns can guess by glance and feeling when a given tavern first began being a tavern. However it may have been pulled about and brought up-to-date in fittings, something of the note set in its early days remains and fixes it. You need only go to the bar of the South London Palace, near the Elephant and Castle, and if you are sensitive, you will find, despite modern drinks and modern dress, that you are back in the period of music-hall's hey-day, and of tall collars, tight trousers and cheroots. And if you want to know what people felt when about to trust themselves to a railway journey in the 'fifties, you need only go to a cavernous bar in a cavernous corner of a certain London terminus. In that dark and monitory hole is preserved all the railway-station atmosphere of that age. It leaves a taste which you can best cleanse by going hot-foot to the bright airy buffet of one of the passenger aerodromes, where you will be as far into the nineteen-thirties as you may hope to get. For at no time do the material features of a social epoch keep up with its spirit. Always they lag some way behind, as we see by our press, our theatre, our parliament, and our cinema. Not even our modern taverns are fully "dressed" with the front rank of life, but we can forgive in the tavern what we cannot forgive in theatre, cinema, or parliament. As for those taverns which are so far behind the procession that they are wearing cravats, gaiters, beaver hats or tie wigs—we would not have them otherwise. We have the affection for them that we have for old arm-chairs, old pipes, old cricket blazers, and first editions with signature H bound upside down.

The tavern indeed can be almost anything it pleases, and we will be pleased by it. The more opportunities it gives us for criticism, the more we criticize, and the more we should miss it if it were not there to criticize. The Puritans of the seventeenth century tried to abolish many things. In the event they abolished only those things which the People did not specially want. They could not abolish the tavern, which *was* wanted. The English People do not want drink for the sake of drink; but they do like, in their hours, to take a drink and to take it in some public place; and the more public that place is, as round a park bandstand, or in a wide-open bar, the better the drink and the better the tone of the people. When plays were performed in flea-pit theatres in back streets, the theatre was patronized mainly by the high and the low. The bourgeois

A TAVERN CAN BE ALMOST ANYTHING

frowned upon it. To them it was only ante-room to hell, and actors and actresses were decoys to ensnare young people beyond the ante-room. But when theatres came into the open, and sprang up all over the West End, they became a middle-class fashion. The bourgeois, and even the Church, found that they could go to the theatre without sin, and actors and actresses were recognized until they became the middle-class deities they are to-day. So with the bar. By degrees it has come out of the contempt of the middle nineteenth century, and to sit half an hour within its walls is no longer a sin. Intelligent people are recognizing that it has justification, not as a drinking-den, but as an occasional resort.

A chair in the tavern, old or new, may not be, as Johnson held, the throne of human felicity, but certainly it arouses more genial talk and impulse than a chair in most other places. And whenever I am invited to a cocktail party in a fashionable loft up a derelict mews, or asked to stand with a glass of sherry against the wall of a luxury flat, because somebody wants the critics to know that it is publishing another book—I think then of the acid and feverish talk I shall hear, and I drop the card into the fire; and, not in bitterness but as a benediction upon all men, even party-givers, I murmur that line by which our lamented G.K.C. first set in literature a long-discountenanced word: the line which is the title of this pamphlet.

www.ingramcontent.com/pod-product-compliance
Lightning Source LLC
Chambersburg PA
CBHW030134260626
47156CB00008B/2945